Ancestry

David Spencer

Copyright © 2021 by David Spencer & Marilyn Spencer

ISBN: 978-1-951670-24-5 (paperback)
ISBN: 978-1-951670-25-2 (ePub)

All rights reserved. No part of this publication may be reproduced, distributed, or transmitted in any form or by any electronic or mechanical means, without the prior written permission of the publisher, except in the case of brief quotations embodied in critical reviews and certain other noncommercial uses permitted by copyright law.

Ordering Information:
For orders and inquiries, please contact:
books@authorsnote360.com
www.authorsnote360.com

Printed in the United States of America

Contents

"Ancestry" 1
Historical Sources for "Ancestry" 2
Sarmatian Tamgas In Polish Heraldry 4
Acknowledgement 6
Foreword 8
Lancers 10
Homeland 12
Romans 14
Visigoths 16
Ancestors 18
The Battle of Hadrianopolis, August 9,378 A.D. 20
Valens the Byzantine 23
A Burial Kurgan of the "Sarmatae" 25
The Battle's "Epilogue" 27
The Romans and the Sarmatians 29
The Descendants of "Sarmacja" 31
"The Theory" 36
"In Alania"-The Sarmatians Beome the Ossetians
of the Caucasus 39
"Polonia" 43
"The Researcher" 46
"The Sarmatian" 53
South Chicago Series 55
"The Golden Stag" Revisited 61
In Summary of, "Ancestry" 68

"Ancestry"

I. The Role of the Sarmatian Alani as allies of the Visigoths against their common enemy the Romans, at the Battle of Hadrianopolis, (Adrianople) in 378 A.D.
II. The Iranian Nomad Sarmatians of the Russian Steppes as ancestors of the Slavic Polish People.

Historical Sources for "Ancestry"

The Royal Assyrian Archives, Re: The Iskuza (Scythian) Prince Partatua (Bartatua) and a Scythian – Assyrian alliance against the Medes. The Royal Assyrian Archives, Re: The Lady Sherua-Eterat, eldest daughter of the Assyrian King Esarhaddon.

The Greek Historian Herodotus (5th Century B.C.) Re: The Scythians

The Greek Historian Strabo, Re: The Sarmatian Roxolani

The Roman poet Ovid, Re: The Sarmatians

The Roman Historian, Ammianus Marcellinus, Re: The Sarmatian Alans (Alani) as allies of the Gothic leader Fritigern, against the Roman Emperor Valens, at the Battle of Hadrianopolis, 378 A.D.

The Roman Historian Tacitus, Re: The Sarmatians, and the Slavic Tribe of the Venedi (Veneti)

Procopius of Caesarea, Re: "Sclaveni" and Antes" (Ancient Slavic Tribes)

The Roman Historian Pliny the Elder, Re: The "Sarmatian Venedi" (Venedi-Sarmatae)

The Historian Jordanes (550 A.D.) Re: The Venedi, the Sclaveni and the Antes (Ancient Slavic Tribes)

The ancient Geographer Claudius Ptolemy, Re: Map of "European Sarmatia"

A book by the Polish Historian Jan Dluglosz (1415- 1480) entitled, *"Annals or Chronicles of the famous Kingdom of Poland"*, Re: Polish "Sarmatism".

A book by the Polish Historian Maciej Miechowita, (1457 – 1523) entitled, "*Tractatus de Duabus Sarmatiis (*or) Treatise of the two Sarmatias", Re: Polish "Sarmatism".

"*The Sarmatians*" by the Polish author Tadeusz Sulimirski, 1970

"*The Golden Stag*" by David Szpejnowski (Spencer) 2015, Re: Scythians

SARMATIAN TAMGAS IN POLISH HERALDRY

Romans :

Valens, the Eastern Roman Emperor
Valentinian I
Gratian the Elder
General Sebastianus
Tribune Equitius
Tribune Potentius
Valerianus, Master of the Stable

Goths :

Fritigern, Gothic leader
Alatheus, and Saphrax, Gothic Chieftains
Athanaric, king of the Thervingian Goths

Ancestors: Sarmatians/Poles

"They keep the cold at bay with skins and breeches. Of the whole body just the face is left, with icicles in the hair – and beards are white with frost below their lips." (The Roman poet Ovid describes Sarmatians, coming across the Danube River.)

Perun, named for the Slavic god of Thunder and Lightning
Dajbog, named for the Slavic god of the Sun Gatalos, a lancer named for an ancient King of the Sarmatians
Stribog, named for the Slavic god and spirit of the Winds, Sky, and Air
Svarog, named for the Slavic god of Fire
Scopasis, son of Perun, named for an ancient King of the Sarmatians
Leyla, Lada, Ziva, Morana, and Zosia: Sarmatian women named for Slavic goddesses
Count Henryk Szpejnowski, a Polish Noble, and member of the Sejm, the Medieval Polish Parliament

(*Note: In Slavic mythology, "Perun" is the highest god of the pantheon and the god of thunder and lightning, just like the Scandanavian "Thor".)

ACKNOWLEDGEMENT

WRITING A BOOK is a journey. It needs imagination, motivation and of course passion.

Publishing my books will not be realized without the support of the people around me.

I'd like to start with Emma Reading (My Wife's Mother) for all the compliments and words of encouragement she has given me. Her words served as my guide to the right direction in writing.

To my very good friends Sam Wilson and Jeff Yelton for all the support they have shown and for pushing me to work on my book.

To our family friends:

- Sandy and Fred Hardy
- Tim and Carol Dionne

Our family is so blessed to have a family friend like you. Always remember that you are always dear to our family.

To my Publisher Author's Note 360, I thank you for showing interest and for believing in my book. I thank the whole team for making this republication possible.

Finally, I dedicate this book to my beautiful and ever supportive wife Marilyn Spencer, the LOVE OF MY LIFE. She's been a huge fan of my books and she supported me all the way. She stood by me in sickness and in health. She's always been the source of my strength and my inspiration. Without her, I'm not sure if I'd be able to finish even a single book. To my beloved Marilyn, I thank you and I love you so much.

FOREWORD

In the days of time forgotten, we rode from the plains of the Caspian Sea, to the northern shore of the Black Sea. In the misty days of our distant past, we rode against them. We lost to Pompey the Great then, 66 years before the Christ. In the time of our forefathers, our kinsmen rode against them again.

They were defeated at Zela then, by their General Julius Caesar, 47 years before the Christ. I am "Perun", a horseman of the Alani, named after our god of thunder and lightning. I ride south across the Danube River, to meet with our allies the Goths, to ride against their Emperor Valens, toward the battle-ground at Hadrianopolis.

LANCERS

ONE THOUSAND YEARS after the fall of the Assyrian Empire, after the deaths of their Kings Esarhaddon and Ashur-Banipal, long after the destruction of the Assyrian city of Nineveh, the Sarmatian horse-bowmen, and lancers like Stribog and Dajbog lived in their house-wagons on the Steppes. The Sarmatian territory was east of the Don River, and south of the Ural Mountains.

Long after the deaths of the Scythian King Partatua and his "half-Assyrian" son Prince Madyas, the Sarmatians had finally driven their "Saka" kinsmen from the Steppes, and into The Crimea. Some Sarmatians were "cattle-breeders". Some tribes were still nomads, though, following their herds from pasture to pasture. Some still collected their tribute of grain and cattle from the "farmer-tribes".

It was possible for Sarmatian war horses to carry their riders for as many as one hundred miles in one day. It was also possible that they could keep up that pace for as many as ten days in a row. On raiding parties, extra horses were used, so that the riders would always have fresh mounts. The animals were small and sturdy, like the ones that would later be called, "Mongol" ponies. Unlike their Scythian forebears, the Sarmatians did not bury a warrior's horse with him, to serve him in an after-life. Yet, their horses were just as important to them.

HOMELAND

IN THE DAYS of the Persian Empire, our people were known to the Greeks and the Romans as, "Massagetae". The Goths, who would later become our allies against the Romans, were called the "Getae". When the Persian King Cyrus the Great invaded our homeland, we were led by our Queen Tomyris.

After the Queen's son Prince Spargapises was captured by the Persians, and committed suicide by stabbing himself, Tomyris took her revenge. She also took the head of Cyrus the Great. The legend says that Queen Tomyris plunged the head of the Persian King into a tub full of blood, saying, "Now Tyrant, have your fill of blood!"

When the Persian King Darius I, called Darius the Great, came to the Steppes to avenge the death of Cyrus, we Sarmatians, led by our King Scopasis, allied ourselves with the forces of the Saka Princes Idanthyrus and Taxacis to drive him out of the steppe-land, back across the Pontus, and back into Persia.

Before the lancers set out to fight the Romans, their families gathered at an encampment of house-wagons on the shore of the Black Sea. As they had always done for centuries, nomadic tribesmen drove their herds to new pastures, all across the Steppes and past the camp.

Perun and his wife waited by their house-wagon with the others. Their son Scopasis, named for an ancient King of the Sauromatae, got ready to join the Alan cavalry as they mounted their horses, took up their lances, and started to thunder away. Lada, the wife of Dajbog was there, with their daughters Ziva and Morana. The woman Zosia prayed for the return of her lover, the Sarmatian lancer Stribog.

O N THE LAST day of his life, Flavius Julius Valens Augustus, son of the Illyrian Gratian the Elder and brother of the Western Emperor Valentinian I, reviewed the troops from Syria, and those that Gratian had sent in, men from Gaul. A few months before the battle, Valens had left Antioch for Constantinople. On the last day of his life, the Roman General Sebastianus, who had just arrived from Italy, looked over his maps and prepared his strategy for the battle against the Goths and the Sarmatian Alans at Hadrianopolis.

On the last day of his life, Equitius, a Tribune and relation of Valens thought of how he had been a prisoner of the Goths, and how he had escaped. On the last day of their lives, Potentius, a Tribune of the Promoti, a branch of the cavalry, and Valerianus, Master of the Stable inspected the herds of the Roman horses.

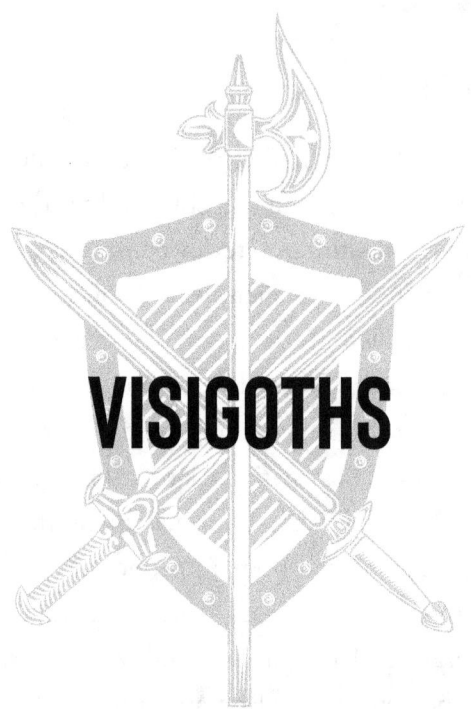

VISIGOTHS

IT WAS SAID that the Goths once lived near the Vistula River, then moved to the southern coast of the Baltic Sea. They also moved to the coast of the Black Sea, where they came into conflict with our Sarmatian Roxolani of the Dneiper River, who they called the "Spali". At that time, they were led by their King Filmer, son of Gadareiks. That was nearly two hundred years ago.

Two years before the battle at Hadrianopolis, Fritigern had received permission from Valens to cross the Danube River, and settle his tribe on Roman lands. Two years before the battle, Valens had sent in his Thracian field army to help Fritigern fight his Gothic rival Athanaric. Now, King Athanaric, who had fought against Fritigern in a civil war, had been defeated by the Huns. The Gothic Greuthungs, who lived in the steppes of the Black Sea, had also fallen to the Huns.

Now, the Goths led by Fritigern were under pressure from the Huns advancing upon Dacia. Two years before the battle, Fritigern had converted to Christianity, holding the same beliefs as the Roman Emperor. Now, Fritigern was in open rebellion against Valens. In preparation for the Battle, the Gothic leaders Saphrax and Alatheus from the steppes of the Black Sea assembled their cavalry and infantry, planning their battle strategies for the approval of their leader, Fritigern.

ANCESTORS

*"Almost all **Alans** are tall and have fair hair, beautiful face, eyesight is if not furious, still is fearsome."*

*(The Roman historian, Ammianus Marcellinus)

*"The **Roxolani** were equipped with helmets and corselets, made of raw ox-hides"*

(*The Greek Historian Strabo)

IN PREPARATION FOR the battle against the Romans, Dajbog and his Alan lancers readied their horses, and their battle equipment. In preparation for the battle, Stribog made sure that his long lance was sturdy enough for combat. The Alan horse-bowmen made sure that their bowstrings were taught, and that their quivers were full of arrows.

In the main Alan encampment of house-wagons, Perun and the Sarmatian Shaman Svarog remembered the defeats suffered at the hands of the Roman Valentinian the Great, brother of Valens. They were ready to take their revenge against Rome as they had done four years before, in the Roman Province of Danubian Pannonia.

THE BATTLE OF HADRIANOPOLIS, AUGUST 9, 378 A.D.

Against the Common Enemy

"Our left wing *had advanced actually up to the wagons, with the intent to push on still further if they were properly supported; but they were deserted by the rest of the cavalry, and so pressed upon by the superior numbers of the enemy, that they were overwhelmed and beaten down ... And by this time such clouds of dust arose that it was scarcely possible to see the sky, which resounded with horrible cries; and in consequence, the darts, which were bearing death on every side, reached their mark, and fell with deadly effect, because no one could see them beforehand so as to guard against them."*

* (The Roman Historian Ammianus Marcellinus) Hadrianoplis – the city named after their Emperor Hadrian. It was near the border of Greece and Bulgaria, in the Roman Province of Thracia. The army of Valens was made up of seven legions, among which were the Legio I Maximiana and imperial auxillaries. The Roman cavalry had mounted archers, just as the Alans did. Valens also had shielded cavalry, and some Arab horsemen. On the morning of the battle, Valens left Hadrianopolis.

He was told that the Gothic camp was north of the city. The Roman Army arrived at the battleground after marching for seven hours. They faced the Gothic camp that had been set up on a hill, and the Goths took up their position in front of their wagon circle.

They then burned the fields in the area, in order to delay the Romans, and give Fritigern enough time to bring in his cavalry. Without orders, a detachment of Romans began the battle. The Roman left-wing reached the circle of wagons, but the Gothic cavalry arrived to support the infantry. The cavalry of the Goths surrounded the Roman troops, who retreated with their heavy armor and long shields, but it was too late.

"In the meantime the Goths had returned with Alatheus and Saphrax, and with them a battalion of **Alans;** *these descending from the mountains*

like a thunderbolt, spread confusion and slaughter among all whom in their rapid charge they came across."* (The Roman historian Ammianus Marcellinus)

At a signal, Dajbog and his lancers charged forward, to be met by a wall of Roman shields and spears. The lancers and their horses were protected by their armor, managing to push their way over the top of a line of defenders. Their long lances found their marks. The hooves of their mounts pounded away, legs clawing through the air.

Stribog and Svarog came with the Alan horse-archers, sending waves of arrows down upon the enemy. They used the old Scythian "mock-retreat" tactic: firing forward, turning their horses to fire back over their shoulders, then charging ahead once more, again and again. Perun, Scopasis and Gatalos rode now, joining with the Gothic cavalry. They crashed into yet another wall of Roman shields, forcing them back. In the charge, the knees of Gatalos's horse buckled, sending him hurling onto the blade of a Roman spear. The relentless massacre of the Romans continued until nightfall. The Emperor himself was abandoned by his guards, and his cavalry deserted him.

After all of the clashing of shields and swords had ceased, when the hand-to hand fighting was over, there were hundreds more Roman bodies on the ground than Gothic ones. When the last arrow had been fired, and the last spear hurled through the air, then the blood-letting finally stopped.

As the last wounded rider was thrown from his fallen horse, the rounding up of the Roman prisoners started. The dead men were thrown into piles, and the dying ones finished off. Valens, the ruler of the Eastern Roman Empire, was nowhere to be found. The combined forces of the Goths and Sarmatians had overwhelmed their enemy completely.

The Sarmatian cavalry from the homeland, including Dajbog, Stribog and Svarog had taken part in the slaughter. They had backed up the Goths with their lancers, and horse-bowmen. In the end, some thirty five Roman Tribunes were slain, along with two thirds of their men. When the battle was over, the Roman casualties numbered in the thousands.

VALENS THE BYZANTINE

"*WHEN THE BARBARIANS ... arrived within fifteen miles from the station of Nike ... the Emperor, with wanton impetuosity, resolved on attacking them instantly, ... what led to such a mistake is unknown – affirmed that their entire body did not exceed ten thousand men.*" *(The Roman historian Ammianus Marcellinus)

The armor and the horses of the Alan lancers were covered with blood, as they rode through the bodies of the Romans. Across the battlefield, the Gothic cavalry of Fritigern rode in silent, sober celebration. The Alan horse-bowmen retrieved their arrows from the defeated, from the fallen.

Dajbog and Stribog pulled the body of the Roman Emperor Valens from a building that the Goths had set on fire. They stood in a circle around the slain ruler for a moment. Then, Svarog planted a sword in the earth that represented the Sarmatian gods of war, Jarilo and Triglav.

The sword looked like a Christian cross, as it stood upright in the ground. Silently, the Alan Shaman Svarog, named for the god of Fire, poured blood over the hilt of the sword. He was joined by the other Alan Chieftains as he knelt in reverence. This ceremony was not only in honor of Jarilo and Triglav, but also in honor of the fallen ruler Valens. His body was not recovered by the Romans. It was "... <u>the beginning of evils for the Roman Empire than and thereafter</u>"* (The Roman historian Ammianus Marcellinus)

A BURIAL KURGAN OF THE "SARMATAE"

Perun, Dajbog, Stribog and the others carried the fallen Sarmatian lancers home to the southern Steppes of the Ural Mountains. Burial "kurgan" mounds were built. This kurgan was that of the slain lancer Gatalos, named for an ancient Sarmatian King. The Shaman Svarog crawled through the underground kurgan entrance, and placed small statues of deer in this tomb. A large bronze cauldron was also buried there, with two griffins pictured on it, "beak-to beak".

Svarog included a small wicker chest, placing it near the head of this warrior. The chest was filled with silver and gold items. Among the other "gifts" for the "after-life" were a wooden box, leather pouches, and the teeth of a horse. There was a large silver mirror with animals on the handle, decorated with the pictures of an eagle and winged bulls. Clothing had plaques sewed into it, showing flowers and a panther, leaping onto the back of an antelope. Pieces of gold leaf were sewn into the breeches, shirt, and scarf. A shawl with fringes on it was clasped with a golden chain. The shirtsleeves were decorated with colored beads. Golden earrings were put on the body. Finally, the Shaman Svarog used stone mixing palettes, iron, gold-covered needles, bone spoons, paints, and pens decorated with animals to tattoo the man.

THE BATTLE'S "EPILOGUE"

THE GOTHS LAID siege to Adrianople. They failed to capture it, being beaten back by the Roman soldiers there at the city walls. Later, the Emperor Theodosius, who succeeded the slain Valens, accepted the Goths as his allies. Between 409 and 453 A.D., the Sarmatian Alani fought alongside two Germanic tribes, the Vandals and the Seuvi. They also fought for Attilla the Hun.

After Hunnic rule had ended, some historians have presented the theory that The Alani became the ancestors of the modern Ossetes of the Caucasus Mountains (North Ossetia-Alania.) Other scholars held that same theory about another pastoral Iranian group, the Scythians. They did not make the distinction between Scythians and Sarmatians, since they were both Iranian stock, nomadic, and closely related. They also contend that some Scythians settled in Dobruja, an area that now includes both modern Bulgaria and Romania.

THE ROMANS AND THE SARMATIANS

Sixteen years Before Christ, the Sarmatians crossed the lower Danube River, but the Roman forces drove them back.

In the year 69 Anno Domini, thousands of Sarmatian Roxolani were defeated by the Roman Legio III Gallica.

In the year 92 Anno Domini, the Sarmatian Iazyges allied themselves with two Germanic Tribes for the first time, in a victory over the Roman Legio XXI Rapax.

In the years 101-102 Anno Domini, The Sarmatian Roxolani allied themselves with the Dacians, in the Roman Emperor Trajan's Dacian War.

In the year 135 Anno Domini, the Sarmatian Alans raided into Media and Armenia. They were driven out of Central Anatolia, by the Roman Governor Arrian.

In the period 167 -180 Anno Domini, the Sarmatian Iazyges were allied with the Germanic tribes for a second time, against the Roman Empire. In the years 173 - 174 Anno Domini, the Sarmatian Iazyges invaded the Roman Province of Pannonia. In a battle that took place on the Danube River, these Sarmatians were defeated by the Roman Emperor Marcus Aurelius. In A.D. 175, peace was made, with thousands of Sarmatian Iazyges being sent to the Roman Province of Brittania, as part of the Emperor's army.

In the years 236-238 Anno Domini, there were more Roman conflicts with the Sarmatian Iazyges. The victorious Roman Emperor Maximinus I is known thereafter as, "Sarmaticus Maximus".

In the year 282 Anno Domini, the Sarmatian Iazyges were defeated by the Roman Emperor Carus, in the Province of Pannonia.

In the year 297 Anno Domini, the Sarmatians fought on the side of the Roman Emperor Galerius, in his war against the Persians.

In the year 378 Anno Domini, the Sarmatian Alan cavalry fought on the side of the Gothic leader Fritigern. At the Battle of Hadrianapolis (Adrianopole) the Roman Army was defeated by a combined force of Goths and Sarmatians, and the Roman Emperor Valens lost his life.

THE DESCENDANTS OF "SARMACJA"

THE SLAVIC TRIBES, called the *"Antes"* and the *"Sclaveni"*, are first mentioned in the Byzantine records of the early 6th century. The Poles, Silesians, and Kashubians are Western Slavic Groups.

These were the words of Procopius of Caesarea:

> *"For these nations, the Sclaveni and the Antae, are not ruled by one man, but they have lived from of old under a democracy, and consequently everything which involves their welfare, whether for good or for ill, is referred to the people.*
>
> *It is also true that in all other matters, practically speaking, these two barbarian peoples have had from ancient times the same institutions and customs. For they believe that one god, the maker of lightning, is alone lord of all things, and they sacrifice to him cattle and all other victims."*
>
> *"They live in pitiful hovels which they set up far apart from one another, but, as a general thing, every man is constantly changing his place of abode. When they enter battle, the majority of them go against their enemy on foot carrying little shields and javelins in their hands, but they never wear corselets. Indeed, some of them do not wear even a shirt or a cloak, but gathering their trousers up as far as to their private parts they enter into battle with their opponents. And both the two peoples have also the same language, an utterly barbarous tongue.*
>
> *Nay further, they do not differ at all from one another in appearance. For they are all exceptionally tall and stalwart men, while their bodies and hair are neither very fair or*

blond, nor indeed do they incline entirely to the dark type, but they are all slightly ruddy in color. And they live a hard life, giving no heed to bodily comforts."

In the ancient Slavic religion there were gods with names like, "Daj-Bog", and "Stri-Bog." In the Polish language, terms like, "Pan Bog", "Bogu" and "Boga" refer to "God." In Polish, "Bog Wojny" translates into, "War god", or "god of war." Is this a coincidence?

The ancient Iranian Sarmatians, nomads of the Russian Steppes, used "tamga" signs and symbols in their religion. The Polish Nobility, or "Szlachta" used these tamgas in the heraldry of prominent families like Kosciesza, Czelusc, Lubicz, and Bielek. Is this yet another coincidence? If you add a "ski" to the name of "Czelusc", you get the modern Polish surname of Czeluski."

It is now the 15th Century A.D. Count Henryk Szpejnowski, a member of the Polish Sejm, the Parliament, is proud of his Sarmatian heritage. His Sarmatian – style "*Karacena*" armor is displayed prominently at his Estate. Ancient Sarmatian "*Tamga*" symbols are used in Count Henryk's family crest, and are displayed upon the ceremonial shield on his wall.

Count Henryk wears a long coat trimmed with fur, called a "*zupan*". He wears thigh-high boots, and carries a saber called the "*szabla*." Like his Sarmatian ancestors, Count Henryk values his stable of horses. In his mind, he sees himself as an armored Alan lancer, riding to battle across the Steppes of the Black Sea.

The idea of the Poles as descendants of the Sarmatians is shared by the nobility of several areas, including the Ukraine and Muscovy. While some of the nobility in the Polish Szlachta class thinks of their ancestors as Turkic, or Crimean Tatars, and somehow superior to their Slavic serfs, Count Henryk does not. He tries to rule the Polish peasants on this Estate as equals.

Unlike other members of the Polish nobility, Count Henryk believes that the King of Poland should not be elected, because his power is limited. The nobility of the Sejm have the right to vote on laws, and can block the King's decisions. They have the right to deny the King's commands, and to oppose him by force of arms. They even have the right to vote on whether or not to maintain a standing army.

The Military would only be called up in the event of an invasion by a foreign enemy, such as the Ottoman Turks. After Jan Sobieski, many of the elected Polish Kings were foreign, not even Polish. There were factions in the Polish nobility that were pro-Russian, pro-German, and pro- Austrian, depending upon which group would benefit them. On a visit to his Estate, in order determine which crops were ready to be harvested, which of the horses in his stable should be put to stud, Count Henryk visited the rude wooden dwelling of one the peasant-farmers, Ignacy. The peasant lived there with wife Ewa, and their many children. These peasants had lived on the Estate all of their lives, as had their parents and grandparents.

As people tied to the land, they would later take a surname that would reflect the name of the Estate that they lived on. Their surname would end in "ski", meaning that they were, indeed, of the land. It would show that they were loyal to their master Count Henryk, and his family.

The Count looked at the stallions in the stable, and tried to imagine them decked out in battle- armor. He couldn't. He tried to envision the stallions being mounted by Sarmatian knights, armed with lances. Again, nothing. There were many who doubted the Noble's theory of "Sarmatism".

They said that Count Henryk and others of his class were merely grasping at straws, trying to prove their ancient heritage. As time went by, even Count Henryk was becoming less and less convinced of the "theory". He looked and the peasants Ignacy and

Ewa, working in the fields alongside the other serfs. Try as he might, he could see no real resemblance to his distant ancestors of the ancient past.

Later on, Henryk sat down at the desk in his study, to try and put his theories into words, and down on paper. He began, "The Indo-European Sarmatians, in ancient times, lived in the area between the Volga River, and the Don River. Also in ancient times, the Sarmatians came into the lands of the Slavs. It is my belief, and the belief of many in our Polish nobility, that we are descended from these Sarmatians. I refer, specifically, to a work by the historian Maciej Miechowita, (1457 – 1523) entitled, _Tractatus de Duabus Sarmatiis_ (or) Treatise of the two Sarmatias. Reference is made, also, to the works of Jan Dluglosz (1415-1480) entitled, _Annals or Chronicles of the famous Kingdom of Poland._ Dluglosz first set forward the premise that the Sarmatians are connected to the pre-history of Poland. Other historians of note in this regard are Bielski, and Kromer."

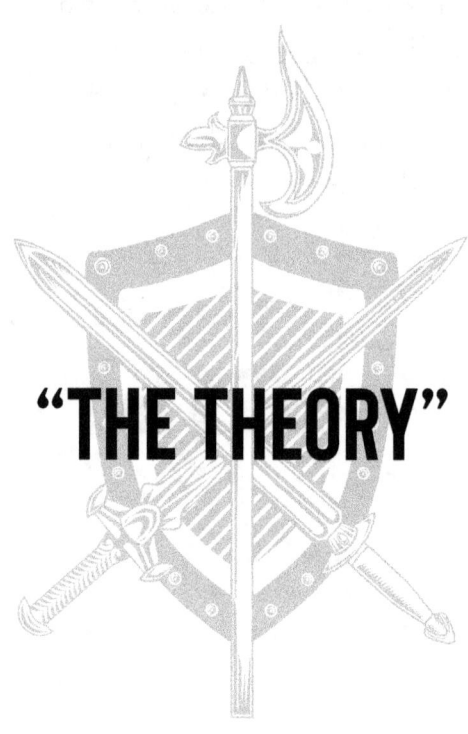

"THE THEORY"

Count Henryk wrote, "Greek and Roman geographers described the "Veneti" as a tribe living along the ***Vistula River***, and what would become to be known today as the "***Bay of Gdansk***". The Roman Historian Tacitus said that he did not know whether to class the ancient tribes of the Peucini, ***Venedi***, and Fenni with the Germans, or with the ***Sarmatians.*** He said that a tribe called the "Bastarnae" were like the Germans in their language, manner of life, mode of settlement and habitation. He went on to say that this tribe had something like the appearance of the ***Sarmatians.*** Tacitus, therefore, did not really know if he was describing German tribes, Sarmatian tribes, or Slavic ones. In other words, he did not know the difference between the three. His Roman point of view, however, classified all of them as "barbarians." He said that the tribe of the Venedi borrowed largely from ***Sarmatian*** ways, but differed from the ***Sarmatians*** in that they had settled houses. Finally, he said that the ***Sarmatians*** lived in wagons, or on horseback. That descriptions would also have applied to their kinsmen the ancient Scythians, who lived in the Crimea, and on the Steppes of the Black Sea. The Romans said that the territory between the Rhine River and the Vistula River was "***Germania***". They said that the lands east of the Vistula made up "***Sarmatia***". The Gothic Historian Jordanes (about 550 A.D.) in his paper "<u>Getica</u>" said that the Veneti were a "populous nation", who dwellings began at the source of the ***Vistula*** River, and occupied "a great expanse of land." He said that the Veneti were the ancestors of both the Sclaveni (Southern Slavs) and the Antes. He said that there were Slavs north of the Dniester River (in Russia) and that the Antes were east of the Slavs. Both the Roman Pliny the Elder and the Historian Jordanes said that a group called the "Sarmatian Venedi" (Venedi-***Sarmatae)*** lived along the Baltic Coast. This is another strong "Sarmatian- Slavic" connection.

Since the Germanic tribes, according to Tacitus, were in such close proximity to the Sarmatians, they must have occupied nearly the same territories, and possibly inter-married. Therefore, it is also possible that some Slavs could be a combination of both the Germanic tribes, and the Sarmatian ones. Since the Germanic Tribes lived in what is now Germany, and the Slavic tribes lived in what is now Poland, it is quite possible, also that Sarmatian tribes invaded Slavic territory, and intermarried with the Slavic tribe that would become the Poles."

"IN ALANIA"-THE SARMATIANS BEOME THE OSSETIANS OF THE CAUCASUS

THE CAUCASUS MOUNTAINS of Eurasia range between Sochi on the north-eastern Shore of the Black Sea, and Baku near the Caspian Sea. There are many ethnic groups in the Caucasus Mountains. In the Northeast, there are the Avars. In the Northwest, there are the Circassians.

Other groups throughout the region include the Azerbaijani, the Chechens, the Georgians, the Armenians, the Ossetians and the Kurds. Of all of these groups, the Kurds and Ossetians are Iranian.

Just as were the nomadic Scythians and Sarmatians from the Black Sea area, and the Steppes.

In the 7th Century, A.D., Mozdok had been part of the Kingdom of the Alans. Its' royal family traced their ancestry back to the nomadic Sarmatian Alani. During the Middle Ages, the town of Mozdok had been menaced by both the Mongols and the Tartars. In 1222 A.D., the Alans and the Turkic Kipchak nomads were allies against a Mongol-Tartar confederation. In the Russo-Turkish War of 1877- 78, there was more armed conflict in the region. Now, in 1942, the whole of the Caucasus was being menaced by Adolf Hitler's Nazi Germany.

The town of Mozdok, on the shore of the Terek River, in the Caucasus had been taken from the Russians the Germans in August. In secret, Vyachaslav was packing supplies and arming himself, getting ready to travel the fifty seven miles south to Vladikavkaz, which was under siege by these German enemies. Mozdok was located in the Mozdoksky District, in the northern Caucasus Mountains. Vladikavkaz, the Ossetian capital, was the industrial center for the region, and of strategic importance. So were the oil fields in Baku.

Vyachaslav met the others of his group, Vitaly, Kazbek and Sergey at the Mozdok Railway Station, hoping to get a train south Mikhail and Eduard, two Georgians from the nearby city of Tbilisi, joined them for this action. A handful of Russian Soldiers came along. The German attack on Vladikavkaz, (Orjonikidze) was the furthest point that the Nazis would reach, crossing the Caucasus.

The Mozdok volunteer group's information was this: A Unit of the 1st Panzer Armee, which was the 13th Panzer Division, was advancing. Also, two reconnaissance squads from the 16th Motorized Infantry Division were on the move. This was made up of eight-wheeler armored cars, a motorcycle platoon, and several trucks.

The Commander of the 13th Panzer Division (Wehrmacht) at the time was General-leutnant Helmut Von der Chevallerie. When Vyachyslav and the others would finally reach the Ossetian capital, it would be clear to them that their main objective was to help destroy as many of the Panzer tanks as they could. Over 1,500 years before, at the Battle of Hadrianapolis, the Samatian Alan cavalry had been allies of the Germanic Goths. Now, their descendants were the enemies of the German Nazis, and their "defensive force".

It was war-time, in the snow. There was no Ossetian "troop – train", so the Mozdok volunteers had to smuggle themselves into the box-car of a freight train. They did not know how far they would get, until they were stopped by snowdrifts, German soldiers, or worse, the Panzer tanks. A few miles down the track, they saw that the railway had been destroyed by the enemy.

After they crawled out of their snow-filled, frozen box car, they found a broken down old truck, that they finally got started. That got them just so far. The rest of the way was made by riding in a famer's horse-cart, and then finally by foot. They were hoping to find some sleds, but had no luck. The snow was no obstacle for the German tanks.

By the time the Mozdok volunteers reached the city, the fighting was already going on. The Germans were trying to take Vladikavkaz, just as the Visigoths had tried to take Hadrianopolis, centuries before. Hitler's forces would fail to take the Ossetian capital in the Caucasus in 1942 A.D., just as Fritigerns' Gothic army had failed to take the capital of Turkish Thrace from the Romans in 378 A.D.

A blast from a Panzer tank shell cut down Vitaly and Kazbek, on the same spot that Mongol horse- archers had overrun in the past. A burst from a German machine gun emplacement ended the lives of the two Georgians, Mikhail and Eduard. Vyachaslav, from the northern Ossetian town of Mozdok, used an anti-tank grenade-launcher on a Panzer tank, on the same spot where his villager ancestors had once fallen to the invading Tartars.

At the end of the fight, the people of the city had been protected by the Soviet Russian troops, who were successful in driving back the Germans. The City of Vladikavkaz in "Sarmatian Alania" did not fall to the Nazi Wehrmacht. Three months later, in February, 1943, the Soviets defeated the Germans at Stalingrad, in the dead of the Russian winter. The Germans were wearing summer uniforms.

"POLONIA"

- On August 5, 1772 Russia, Prussia and Austria signed a treaty that partitioned Poland. It was ratified by the Polish Sejm (legislature.)
- On January 23, 1793 Russia and Prussia agreed upon the Second Partition of Poland after the Polish Sejm was surrounded by Russian troops.
- On October 24, 1795 Russia, Prussia and Austria concluded an agreement that resulted in the Third Partition of Poland.
- Under the French Emperor Napoleon Bonaparte, the "Duchy of Warsaw" was created in 1807. In 1809, the Polish Lancers of the Vistula Region were part of The "Polish Legions" that were an army in exile, under French command. They took part in Napoleon's victorious war against Austria.
- In 1868 Ignacy Szpejnowski was born in Bydgoszcz (German Bromberg) in northern Poland, on the Brda and Vistula Rivers. Ignacy and his wife Ewa Warzynski have ten children, one of which is named Jozef. Jozef sailed to America from the seaport of Gdansk. Ignacy died in 1959 at the age of 91, and was buried in Bydgoszcz.
- Another one of Ignacy's sons, Antoni, is an American volunteer in a cavalry unit of The "Armia Polska We Francyi" (The Polish Legion in France – also called "Haller's Army", or the "Blue Army") that defeated the Russian Red Army at the Battle of Warsaw, in 1920. It was called, "The Miracle on the Vistula".
- In 1923, Henry H. Szpejnowski, son of the Polish immigrant Jozef Szpejnowski is born in Chicago. He serves in France in World War II, under the command of General Eisenhower. His Unit is the 165th General Hospital. His brother John Szpejnowski is awarded the Bronze Star, for action against the Japanese in the Philippines.
- Aleksander Szpejnowski was a member of the Polish Army during the September, 1939 campaign. Because of the pact between Hitler and Stalin, Poland was attacked from the west by Germany, and from the east by Soviet Russia at the same time. After Poland's defeat, Aleksander and many other Polish

soldiers are forced into exile, sent by Stalin to Siberia. After the war, Aleksander emigrates to Yorkshire in England.

- The No. 303 Polish Fighter Squadron was one of 16 Polish Squadrons in the British Royal Air Force in World War Two. 141 Polish pilots took part in the Battle of Britain, helping to defeat the German Luftwaffe. Of those, 29 were killed.
- In 1947, David Szpejowski was born in Chicago. He is the son of Henry, the Grandson of Jozef, and the Great-Grandson of Ignacy (Ignatius) from Bydgoszcz.

Example of some words in the Sarmatian Language:

Were the Scythians and Sarmatians Iranian, or were they, in fact, "Turkic", from the area of Anatolia?

Shivda
vinza
kalanda
minogama
Iyda
yakutalima
batama
Nuffasha
zinzama
ohuto
Kopotso
kopotsam
kopotsama
Yabudala
vikgaza
meyda
patstso
sholda
Koffudamo
shiraffo
stsohalemo

"THE RESEARCHER"

I N 1974, DAVID Szpejnowski was looking for information for his story, "*The Golden Stag*", at the Indiana University Library. His interest in Scythians had begun years earlier, because they were ancient Russians. As a young man, he saw many similarities between the Scythians and American Indians. Like the Indians, they rode on horseback, using bows and arrows as their weapons. Like the Indians, they lived in tents. As he learned from reading the "*Histories of Herodotus*", they even took scalps.

For centuries, the main source of information about the Scythians was the Greek historian Herodotus (5th Century B.C.) He wrote about their origins, their customs, their religion, their various tribes, and their repulsion of an invasion by the Persians. Since there were Greek colonies on the Black Sea, (Olbia, Sinope) it makes sense that Herodotus obtained his information directly from the Scythians themselves.

{Herodotus 1.103} *"A battle was fought, in which the Assyrians suffered a defeat, and Cyaxares had already begun the siege of the place, when a numerous horde of* **Scyths***, under their king* **Madyes***, son of* **Prtotohyes***, burst into Asia in pursuit of the Cimmerians whom they had driven out of Europe, and entered the Median territory."*

{Herodotus 1.104} *"The* **Scythians***, having thus invaded Media, were opposed by the Medes, who gave them battle, but, being defeated, lost their empire. The* **Scythians** *became masters of Asia".*

For David, the theories that the Scythian Bartatua (the "Prtotohyes" of Herodotus) married a daughter of the Assyrian King Esarhaddon, and that their son was the Scythian King Madyes seemed credible. Where did the idea come from, that the Scythians and the Assyrians formed a "wedding- alliance"? The answer comes in a quote from King Esarhaddon, in the Royal Assyrian archives:

"*Regarding Partatua, King of the Iskuza (Scythians) who has just sent his ambassador to Esarhaddon, King of Assyria, about q princess I ask you, Shamash, (Sun-God)*

> great lord, if Esarhaddon gives a princess to Partatua King of the Iskuza for a wife, whether Partatua will observe and keep his oath to Esarhaddon, King of Assyria?"

But, who was the Assyrian Princess? Which daughter of Esarhaddon was it? The answer came in a letter to the wife of the Assyrian Prince Ashur- Banipal, from his sister, Sherua – Eterat:

> "... while you are only a daughter- in- law, the lady of the house of Ashur-Banipal, the eldest son of the King born in the official residence of Esarhaddon, King of Assyria... after all, I, **Sherua-Eterat**, (Goddess - Sherua -is -the –one- who -saves) amthe **eldest daughter** born in the official residence to Esarhaddon, the great and legitimate King, King of the world, King of Assyria".

"So now", thought David, "I know who the Assyrian Princess was." This was the only recorded name that he could find. It made sense, because she was the eldest daughter of King Esarhaddon.

So, Sherua-Eterat must have been the wife of the Scythian King Partatua (Bartatua.) So, Sherua- Eterat must have been the mother of the Scythian Prince Madyes.

While researching the Scythians, David learned that they were related to another nomadic Iranian group, the Sarmatians. And he also learned that there was a theory that the Sarmatians were ancestors of the Poles. Since his background was Polish, this theory intrigued him.

In the same section of the Library as the Histories of Herodotus, David found *"The Sarmatians* "(Ancient Peoples and Places, Vol. 73) written in 1970 by Tadeusz Sulimirski, a Polish historian and archaeologist. Further research showed that a Sarmatian group called the "Alans", or, "Alani" had been enemies of the Roman Empire for hundreds of years. It was learned that the Alans had been allies of the Goths against the Romans at the Battle of Hadrianopolis, in 378 A.D.

In that battle, the Eastern Roman Emperor had lost his life.

How do we know what the Alans looked like? The answer came in a quote from a Roman historian, Ammianus Marcellinus):

> *"Almost all **Alans** are tall and have fair hair, beautiful face, eyesight is if not furious, still is fearsome."* *(The Roman historian, Ammianus Marcellinus)

How do we know that there were Sarmatians at the battle of Hadrianopolis? The answer came in another quote from Ammianus Marcellinus):

> *"In the meantime the Goths had returned with Alatheus and Saphrax, and with them a battalion of **Alans**; these descending from the mountains like a thunderbolt, spread confusion and slaughter among all whom in their rapid charge they came across."* *(The Roman historian Ammianus Marcellinus)

While researching the Sarmatians further, David learned:

1. _Tamgas_ were primitive Sarmatian religious symbols. _Tamgas_ were, in fact, used in the Heraldry of the Medieval Polish nobility.
2. Sarmatian style armor, called, "_Karacena_" was used by the Medieval Polish military.
3. The Polish nobility carried sabers called, "_Szablas_".
4. The Polish nobility wore a Sarmatian style robe, called a "_Kontusz_. They also wore a long coat trimmed with fur, called a "_Zupan_"
5. A book by Jan Dluglosz (1415-1480) entitled, "_Annals or Chronicles of the famous Kingdom of Poland_" concentrated upon the "Sarmatian" concepts.

6. Another book by the historian Maciej Miechowita, (1457 – 1523) entitled, "_Tr actatus de Duabus Sarmatiis (_or) Treatise of the two Sarmatias" also centered on this theory of "Sarmatism".
7. The name "_Sarmacja_" became synonymous with Poland, during the era of _"Sarmatism"_ in Medieval Poland.

The Slavic tribes, called the _"Antes"_ and the "_Sclaveni_", are first mentioned in the Byzantine records of the early 6th century The Poles, Silesians, and Kashubians are Western Slavic Groups.

These were the words of Procopius of Caesarea:

> _"For these nations, the Sclaveni and the Antae, are not ruled by one man, but they have lived from of old under a democracy, and consequently everything which involves their welfare, whether for good or for ill, is referred to the people._
>
> _It is also true that in all other matters, practically speaking, these two barbarian peoples have had from ancient times the same institutions and customs. For they believe that one god, the maker of lightning, is alone lord of all things, and they sacrifice to him cattle and all other victims."_
>
> _"They live in pitiful hovels which they set up far apart from one another, but, as a general thing, every man is constantly changing his place of abode. When they enter battle, the majority of them go against their enemy on foot carrying little shields and javelins in their hands, but they never wear corselets. Indeed, some of them do not wear even a shirt or a cloak, but gathering their trousers up as far as to their private parts they enter into battle with their opponents. And both the two peoples have also the same language, an utterly barbarous tongue._

Nay further, they do not differ at all from one another in appearance. For they are all exceptionally tall and stalwart men, while their bodies and hair are neither very fair or blond, nor indeed do they incline entirely to the dark type, but they are all slightly ruddy in color. And they live a hard life, giving no heed to bodily comforts."

"*Here Suebia ends. I do not know whether to class the tribes of the Peucini, Venedi, and Fenni with the Germans or with the* **Sarmatians.** *The Peucini, however, who are sometimes called Bastarnae, are like Germans in their language, manner of life, and mode of settlement and habitation. Squalor is universal among them and their nobles are indolent. Mixed marriages are giving them something of the repulsive appearance of the* **Sarmatians...** *The Veneti have borrowed largely from* **Sarmatian** *ways; their plundering forays take them all over the wooded and mountainous country that rises between the Peucini and the Fenni. Nevertheless, they are to be classed as Germani, for they have settled houses, carry shields and are fond of travelling fast on foot; in all these respects they differ from the* **Sarmatians,** *who live in wagons or on horseback."*

(*The Roman Historian Tacitus)

The ancient geographer Claudius Ptolemy, in his description of "European Sarmatia", listed forty one sets of map coordinates, twenty two towns, and sixty one group names, including:

- The Aorsi (Avars)
- Rhoxolani (Sarmatian Roxolani)
- Melanchaeni (The Scythian "Black Robes" from the History of Herodotus
- Sarmatian Iazyges

- Sarmatian Alani
- Bodini (The Scythian "Budini" from the History of Herodotus.)
- The Scythian Agathyrsi from the History of Herodotus

In the ancient Slavic religion there were gods with names like, "Daj-Bog", and "Stri-Bog." In the Polish language, terms like, "Pan Bog", "Bogu" and "Boga" refer to "God." In Polish, "Bog Wojny" translates into, "War god", or "god of war." Is this a coincidence?

"THE SARMATIAN"

I

In the days of time forgotten
we rode from the plains of the Caspian Sea,
to the northern shore of the Black Sea.
In the misty days of our distant past,
we rode against them ...
we lost to Pompey the Great then,
66 years before the Christ.

II

In the time of our fore-fathers,
our kinsmen rode against them again ...
they were defeated at Zela then,
by their General Julius Caesar,
47 years before the Christ.

III

I am "Perun", a horseman of the Alani,
named after our god of thunder and lightning ...
I ride south across the Danube River,
to meet with our allies the Goths,
to ride against their Emperor Valens,
toward the battle-ground at Hadrianopolis.

SOUTH CHICAGO SERIES

Slavic Easter
By David Spencer

In the shape of a Cross on the wall,
leaves from the palms of Palm Sunday
are nailed, as if to ward off spirits...
baskets of food to Easter Mass,
like offerings to a temple.
The procession bends down,
at the end of the mass
to kiss the wound
in the side of the Crucifix.

Boy on a Pony
By David Spencer

When South Chicago
was still a Polish Village,
as the ancient scissors sharpener
wheels his grindstone down the street,
as the bearded scissors sharpener
wheels his grindstone down the street...
a compulsory ritual, almost ceremonial
like posing for a portrait,
like the offspring of royalty ...
a five year old, squinting in the sun
smiling a child's smile, mounted on a pony
a brown and white pony, half asleep
staring dumbly into oblivion.
A cowboy hat, and a faded red kerchief
worn by dozens of five-year-olds
as the ancient scissors sharpener

wheels his grindstone down the street,
as the bearded scissors sharpener
wheels his grindstone down the street.

In the Shadow of the Skyway
By David Spencer

In the shadow of the Skyway,
distant memories hang on:
of sunny days, rainy days, ancient days -
days of misty rays of sunlight
filtering through clouds
of steel-mill smoke...
past masses, traditions, holiday meals,
people long ago forgotten, moved away,
left behind...
Now, that world exists in memories,
lives on only in the mind;
When those who lived in the South Side
in the 40's, 50's, 60's are all gone
the South Chicago Skyway
will be just a bridge for traffic,
nothing in the past, nothing beyond.

Polish Village
By David Spencer

(South Chicago, 1953)
The warm summer night - trees shining,
rustling gently in the streetlight...
And the Steel Mill, always the Mill -
looming large, a gray metal mountain
blocking out the sun.

The flashing neon bubbles, floating,
rising from the champagne glass
in the window of the bar on the corner...

or just lying on a bed on a hot summer night,
staring blankly at the reflection
of the ceiling light in the window,
or the moth fluttering near the light,
or the pattern of the bricks
of the house crowded next door.
And the Steel Mill, always the Mill -
looming large, a gray metal mountain
blocking out the sun.

Uncle Tony
By David Spencer

Eighty years old, and danced the polka ...
the retired mill guard
sat watching wrestling from Milwaukee
with his can of "Old Style",
alone in his room on East 79th Place,
across the Illinois Central tracks,
near Uncle Johnny the crane operator,
and Uncle Eddie the mill guard,
and Uncle Chester the Goldblatt's butcher...
a few blocks from St. Michael's,
a medieval castle
towering over a peasant village...
Eighty years old, and danced the polka
my Great Uncle Tony.

Eastern European Photograph
By David Spencer

They are posed, in the cavernous doorway
of a picturesque old wooden dwelling,
like a scene
from the heart of the German Black Forest,
the Gingerbread House of Hansel & Gretel.
His leathery peasant hands,
long and bony with age,
are like his bony wooden cane,
dried out and hardened by time…
her wizened peasant face,
sunken and wrinkled with age…
hand folded, eyes hooded
stares coldly ahead,
into a cold camera lens.
Dressed in simple peasant clothes,
their simple peasant shoes
are planted on their peasants' porch,
on photographic paper.

South Chicago
By David Spencer

Tall brick buildings,
with attics and basements,
brown brick buildings, built in the 30s
surround the god, "Steel Mill",
engulf the church, St Michael's Cathedral,
towering like a medieval castle
over a peasant village.
South shore tracks of the Illinois Central,

olive drab metal, tan rattan seats
clunking, jolting through South Chicago …
83rd Street to Roosevelt Road,
steep zig-zag wooden stairs
blackened with age.
Get up in the morning, work in the Mill,
go home when you're through,
or go to the tavern.
Get up in the morning, work in the Mill,
rise and kneel in the Church on Sunday.

Moments in Memory, 1953
By David Spencer

Imagination, stories were the world
combined with church, and school, and relatives.
Fireworks on a moonlit summer shore,
witches burned in effigy in autumn.
Old World food, and speech, and customs
Old world music,
dreams, and people.
Exploratory walks, alone.
A black straw witch, perched on a broomstick,
hurled into the fire with shout,
burned to ashes with a cheer
and the child, dressed up as a pirate,
rouge and a bandana
the child stands silently, watching
etching the moment in memory.

"THE GOLDEN STAG" REVISITED

"The Scythians were displaced on the Russian Steppes by their nomadic kinsmen, the Sarmatae, about 110 B.C. These Sarmatian tribesmen, who were both the allies and the enemies of the Romans, are believed to be the ancestors of the Poles."

The Story, "*The Golden Stag*" takes place circa 673 B.C., on the Steppes of Southern Russia, and in the Assyrian capital of Nineveh. It centers on the marriage-alliance between the daughter of the Assyrian King Esarhaddon, and the Scythian (ancient Iranian) King Bartatua. The common enemy of the Assyrians and the Scythians of the time are the Medes (ancient Persians.)

"In 1947, a team of Russian archaeologists excavated an ancient tomb in what had been a northern province of the Assyrian Empire. That same year, the Dead Sea Scrolls had been found in the Qumran caves of Israel. The Russian site was at Ziwiyeh, in the territory of a mountain people the Assyrians had called the Mannai. They were known to historians as the Mannaeans.

The Archaeologists had come to this spot after working at several sites in Soviet Armenia. In the time of the Assyrians, Armenia was called, "Urartu". The team had found extensive evidence of nomadic Scythian attacks and devastation at the Armenian digs. Now, they were working near the border of Azerbaijan and Kurdistan, west of Lake Urmia.

Stefan Sulimirsky of the University of Moscow supervised the digging. Henryk Szpejnowski from the University of Krakow in Poland carefully brushed off the objects that would be sent to the Hermitage Museum.

Along with the golden artifacts left behind by a race of nomad warriors from the distant past, the scientists discovered a leather scroll in a bronze box. Written on the scroll were words in an ancient Indo-European language known to the archaeologists. It was the story of a people long supposed to have no record of their own. It was the story of their existence on the Russian Steppes, and in the Crimea. Combined with information from the Assyrian Archives, it provided a clearer picture of their role in history.

The Polish scientist made his first note: *This story began 674 years before the birth of Christ...*

... At this point, Stefan Sulimirsky took a break from analyzing the text of the scroll. It was painstaking work, using a magnifying glass to make out some of the characters. Stan himself was an Assyriologist, and an expert in Central Asian languages. Henryk had specialized in Eastern European dialects at the University of Krakow.

When neither of them could decipher a word or a passage, they referred to an old German textbook from the 1890's. While Henryk took over examining the scroll, his Russian partner Stefan catalogued a find from the day's dig. It was a golden stag, unbroken and beautiful. He thought that possibly it had been made by one of the Greek colonists of the Black Sea area, about 500 B.C.

If so, it had come either from Olbia or Sinope. This site was important to Stefan, because he had long considered himself to be a descendant of the Nomadic Scythians. That is why he became interested in archaeology in the first place. It seemed to him now that he was looking straight into the face of his ancestry.

He wrote, *The article is an ornament, used in the Scythian religion. The hind quarters of this golden animal are raised slightly, with the back legs pointing forward. The front legs are folded under the muscular metal body of the stag, and pointed backwards, giving the illusion of movement. The front and back hooves meet under the sculpture, welded together.*

The stylized curling row representing the antlers of the stag run all the way from the rear of its body to the top of its head. The neck is elongated, and the head is lifted up, adding to the illusion of motion of flight. After making his notes, Sulimirsky went back to the scroll...

The Polish Archaeologist Henryk Szpejnowski lit the lantern in his tent. It was the last evening, at the end of the dig. He carefully placed the ancient scroll in a wooden crate, and made his final notes: *It is now the year 1947 A.D. Over 2500 years have gone by since the Scythian Shaman left the scroll here at Ziwiyeh. Twenty-one years after the Scytho-Assyrian alliance King Ashur-Banipal, would enlist the help of the nomad Prince Madyas against the Median King Phraortes and his allies.*

That Prince was the son of Bartatua and the Assyrian Princess; he would fight against the Madai and the Gimirrai, handing them a crushing defeat. Twelve years after the death of his Assyrian Uncle Ashur-Banipal, Madyas would join with the Medes and Babylonians to destroy the Royal Assyrian city. There was a span of only fifty-two years between the time of the wedding- alliance, and the fall of Nineveh.

Henryk put down his notepad. He gave a last look at the scroll of Exampaeus, and the Royal Golden Stag."

"Steppe Clans"

I

The Sound was barely audible,
like the gentle noise
made by the metal horse-trappings
as the muscles of the animals
lurched slowly forward
with the movement of their hooves.
In late autumn,
the tall feather - grass of the Steppes
was dried out,
giving way to the hooves unwillingly...
The Nomad Saka Cavalry
came upon a huge burial kurgan,
a mound of earth worn away by time.

II

The top layer of the earthen mound
had been blown away
by the wind of the Steppes,
exposing the death-guard
of a fallen Saka king.
The riders who were still erect
sat upon the saddled bones
of their horses ...
tattered remnants of clothing
that still clung to the bodies

of the death-guard fluttered in the wind.
Small silver bells hung from their horses,
from the worn leather death-masks
of their mounts
as the bells moved with the wind,
they played a hollow, haunting tune.

III

These were the words of the Scythian Shaman
Exampaeus:

At those Royal gates of Nineveh,
I stood as though transfixed;
spellbound looking up, ever higher
to the great stone statues
of the sacred Winged Bulls, the Lamassi
The winged Lamassu had long muscular legs,
the hooves of bulls, the paws of lions
like powerful animals in their stride.
The great stone wings made the gods look
as though they were in flight,
like some kind of giant eagles.
High above the wings, the rock hard gods
wore the tall Royal Assyrian crowns.
The winged gods
had the faces of the kings of Ashur...
the long, stony beards combined
the strength of the bulls and the lions
with the deity
of the Royal House of Assyria.

IV

Dawn on the northern shore,
on the ancient shore of the Black Sea.
Tent-Nomads take their herds to pasture,
as a flowing sea of Nomad Horse-Bowmen
rides the flowing Steppe-lands.
In the royal tent of the Nomad Chieftain,
enemy skulls filled with molten gold
rest on the colorful carpet,
on the red and gold woven carpet
decorated with royal Golden Stags.
The Chieftain's horse, a small Mongol pony
has enemy scalps, hanging from its bridle.
The Nomad god of the sun, Oetosyrus
gleams in the dawn from the royal shield,
gleams in the dawn from the sacred Golden Stag.
Dusk on the northern shore,
on the ancient shore of the Black Sea.
The Nomads, a flowing sea of ox-drawn
house-wagons,
of black felt tents, vanish
in the frozen sea of time.

IN SUMMARY OF, "ANCESTRY"

IN "_FOREWORD_", it is explained that the Sarmatians came from the plains of the Caspian Sea, in Central Asia. It is related that the Sarmatians and the Romans had conflicts in 66 B.C., and also in 47 B.C. The Character "Perun" is introduced as a horseman of the Sarmatian Alani. (Alans) "Perun" was actually the name of the Slavic god of thunder and lightning. Using this name is intended to show a connection between the Sarmatians and the Slavs. Perun says that he and the other Alans are allied with the Germanic Goths, and that there will be a battle against the Roman Emperor Valens at Hadrianopolis. (Adrianapolis)

In "_Lancers_", the Slavic deity names of "Stribog" and "Dajbog" are used for Sarmatian warriors. The territory occupied by the Sarmatians is discussed (east of the Don River and south of the Ural Mountains.) That is roughly the same area held by the Scythians, who were driven out of the Steppes and the Crimea by the Sarmatians. It is mentioned that the Sarmatians lived in house-wagons, just as the Scythians did.

In "_Homeland_", the text explains that the Sarmatians were once known as the "Massagetae", and that the Goths had once been called the "Getae". These names were used by the Greek Historian Herodotus, (5th Century B.C.) in his description of the many different tribes that inhabited Scythia. The text also says that the Scythian Princes Idanthyrus and Taxacis had been allied with the Sarmatian King Scopasis against the Persian King Darius I (513 B.C.) This was also recorded by Herodotus.

In "_Romans_" the names of the various members of the Roman Army who would lose their lives at the Battle of Hadrianaopolis in 378A.D. are listed. These are: The Roman Emperor Valens, his General Sebastianus, the Tribune Equitus, the Tribune Potentius, and Valerianus, who was the "Master of the Stable."

In "_Visigoths_" it is told that that this Gothic tribe had once lived by the Vistula River (in what is now Poland) but had migrated to the southern coast of the Baltic Sea. They also travelled to the coast of the

Black Sea where they came into contact with the Sarmatian Roxolani of the Dneiper River, whom they called the "Spali". Two years before the Battle of Hadrianopolis, the Gothic leader Fritigern was in open rebellion against the Roman Emperor Valens.

In "*Ancestors*", the Sarmatian Shaman Svorog (also the name of a Slavic deity) is introduced. Svarog remembers the Sarmatian defeats at the hands of the Roman Emperor Valentinian the Great, who is the brother of Valens. Svarog is anxious for another triumph against Rome, which had occurred four years earlier in the Roman Province of Danubian Pannonia.

He probably had no idea that the Eastern Roman Emperor Valens would lose his life against the combined forces of his Sarmatian Alans, and the Germanic Visigoths. He prayed to his gods (Perun, Stribog. Dajbog, Jarilo, Triglav) for victory against the Romans of course, but the death of Valens would have exceeded his greatest expectations. He would have given thanks to his gods.

The Battle of Hadrianopolis, 378 A.D., is best covered by three quotes by the Roman Historian Ammianus Marcellinius:

1. *"When the barbarians … arrived within fifteen miles from the station of Nike … the Emperor, with wanton impetuosity, resolved on attacking them instantly, … what led to such a mistake is unknown – affirmed that their entire body did not exceed ten thousand men."*

2. *"Our left wing had advanced actually up to the wagons, with the intent to push on still further if they were properly supported; but they were deserted by the rest of the cavalry, and so pressed upon by the superior numbers of the enemy, that they were overwhelmed and beaten down … And by this time such clouds of dust arose that it was scarcely possible to see the sky, which resounded with horrible cries; and in consequence, the darts, which were bearing death on every side, reached their mark, and fell with deadly effect, because no one could see them beforehand so as to guard against them."*

3. *"In the meantime the Goths had returned with Alatheus and Saphrax, and with them a battalion of **Alans**; these descending from the mountains like a thunderbolt, spread confusion and slaughter among all whom in their rapid charge they came across."*

In "<u>Valens the Byzantine</u>" a fictional account of the death of Valens is presented:

"Dajbog and Stribog pulled the body of the Roman Emperor Valens from a building that the Goths had set on fire. They stood in a circle around the slain ruler for a moment. Then, Svarog planted a sword in the earth that represented the Sarmatian gods of war, Jarilo and Triglav. The sword looked like a Christian cross, as it stood upright in the ground. Silently, the Alan Shaman Svarog, named for the god of Fire, poured blood over the hilt of the sword. He was joined by the other Alan Chieftains as he knelt in reverence. This ceremony was not only in honor of Jarilo and Triglav, but also in honor of the fallen ruler Valens. His body was not recovered by the Romans."

<u>A Burial Kurgan of the "Sarmatae"</u> would be nearly identical to a Scythian grave. This is understandable, since both nomadic groups were probably of Iranian (or possibly Turkic?) origins. Both were closely related ethnically, and both occupied the same geographic areas from about 1500 B.C. to 110 A.D. "Kurgans" like this were discovered by archaeologists, and their contents were meticulously recorded:

"Perun, Dajbog, Stribog and the others carried the fallen Sarmatian lancers home to the southern Steppes of the Ural Mountains. Burial "kurgan" mounds were built. This kurgan was that of the slain lancer Gatalos, named for an ancient Sarmatian King. The Shaman Svarog crawled through the underground kurgan entrance, and placed small statues of deer in this tomb. A large bronze cauldron was also buried there, with two griffins pictured on it, "beak-to beak".

Svarog included a small wicker chest, placing it near the head of this warrior. The chest was filled with silver and gold items. Among the other "gifts" for the "after-life" were a wooden box, leather pouches, and the teeth of a horse. There was a large silver mirror with animals on the handle, decorated with the pictures of an eagle and winged bulls. Clothing had plaques sewed into it, showing flowers and a panther, leaping onto the back of an antelope. Pieces of gold leaf were sewn into the breeches, shirt, and scarf. A shawl with fringes on it was clasped with a golden chain. The shirtsleeves were decorated with colored beads. Golden earrings were put on the body. Finally, the Shaman Svarog used stone mixing palettes, iron, gold-covered needles, bone spoons, paints, and pens decorated with animals to tattoo the man."

The Romans and Sarmatians covers a period between 16 B.C., and 378 A.D., when the Battle of Hadrianoplis occurred. Many times, the Sarmatian tribes were defeated by the Romans. In 175 A.D., after a defeat, Sarmatian Iazgyes were sent to the Roman Province of Brittania, as part of the Emperor's Army. Sometimes, the Sarmatians allied themselves with the Germanic tribes, and were victorious against the Romans. Sometimes, they even fought on the side of the Romans.

In the Medieval era of "Sarmatism", the Polish name for "Sarmatia" was "Sarmacja". The Second part of, *"Ancestry",* beginning with, *The Descendants of Sarmacja"* explores the theory (and it is a **theory**) that the Polish people were descended from the ancient nomadic Sarmatians of the Russian Steppes. It is important to note that this theory was presented by the Polish Nobility, The Polish Clergy, and the Polish Intelligentsia, not the common people.

The theory, explained by the fictional Count Henryk Szpejnowski of the Polish *Szlachta*, supports this point of view:

"It is now the 15th Century A.D. Count Henryk Szpejnowski, a member of the Polish Sejm, the Parliament, is proud of his Sarmatian heritage. His Sarmatian – style "*Karacena*" armor is displayed prominently at his Estate. Ancient Sarmatian "*Tamga*" symbols are used in Count Henryk's family crest, and are displayed upon the ceremonial shield on his wall.

Count Henryk wears a long coat trimmed with fur, called a "*zupan*". He wears thigh-high boots, and carries a saber called the "_szabla_." Like his Sarmatian ancestors, Count Henryk values his stable of horses. In his mind, he sees himself as an armored Alan lancer, riding to battle across the Steppes of the Black Sea.

The idea of the Poles as descendants of the Sarmatians is shared by the nobility of several areas, including the Ukraine and Muscovy. While some of the nobility in the Polish Szlachta class thinks of their ancestors as Turkic, or Crimean Tatars, and somehow superior to their Slavic serfs.

Count Henryk sat down at the desk in his study, to try and put his theories into words, and down on paper. He began, "The Indo-European Sarmatians, in ancient times, lived in the area between the Volga River, and the Don River. Also in ancient times, the Sarmatians came into the lands of the Slavs. It is my belief, and the belief of many in our Polish nobility, that we are descended from these Sarmatians.

I refer, specifically, to a work by the historian Maciej Miechowita, (1457 – 1523) entitled, _Tractatus de Duabus Sarmatiis (or)_ Treatise of the two Sarmatias. Reference is made, also, to the works of Jan Dluglosz (1415-1480) entitled, _Annals or Chronicles of the famous Kingdom of Poland._ Dluglosz first set forward the premise that the Sarmatians are connected to the pre-history of Poland. Other historians of note in this regard are Bielski, and Kromer. Count Henryk wrote, "Greek and Roman geographers described the "Veneti" as a tribe living along the **Vistula River**, and what would become to be known today as the "**Bay of Gdansk**". The Roman Historian Tacitus said that he did not know whether to class the ancient tribes of the Peucini, **Venedi,** and Fenni with the Germans, or with the **Sarmatians.** He said that a tribe called the "Bastarnae" were like the Germans in their language, manner of life, mode of settlement and habitation. He went on to say that this tribe had something like the appearance of the **Sarmatians.**

Tacitus, therefore, did not really know if he was describing German tribes, Sarmatian tribes, or Slavic ones. In other words, he did not know the difference between the three. His Roman point of view, however, classified all of them as "barbarians." He said that the tribe of the Venedi borrowed largely from **Sarmatian** ways, but differed from the **Sarmatians** in that they had settled houses. Finally, he said that the **Sarmatians** lived in wagons, or on horseback. That descriptions would also have applied to their kinsmen the ancient Scythians, who lived in the Crimea, and on the Steppes of the Black Sea. The Romans said that the territory between the Rhine River and the Vistula River was "*Germania*". They said that the lands east of the Vistula made up "*Sarmatia*". The Gothic Historian Jordanes (about 550 A.D.) in his paper "*Getica*" said that the Veneti were a "populous nation", who dwellings began at the source of the **Vistula** River, and occupied "a great expanse of land." He said that the Veneti were the ancestors of both the Sclaveni (Southern Slavs) and the Antes. He said that there were Slavs north of the Dniester River (in Russia) and that the Antes were east of the Slavs. Both the Roman Pliny the Elder and the Historian Jordanes said that a group called the "Sarmatian Venedi" (Venedi-*Sarmatae*) lived along the Baltic Coast. This is another strong "Sarmatian- Slavic" connection.

Since the Germanic tribes, according to Tacitus, were in such close proximity to the Sarmatians, they must have occupied nearly the same territories, and possibly inter-married. Therefore, it is also possible that some Slavs could be a combination of both the Germanic Tribes, and the Sarmatian ones. Since the Germanic Tribes lived in what is now Germany, and the Slavic Tribes lived in what is now Poland, it is possible that the Germans and Slavs inter- married. It is quite possible, also that Sarmatian Tribes invaded Slavic territory, and inter-married with the Slavic Tribe that would become the Poles."

www.ingramcontent.com/pod-product-compliance
Lightning Source LLC
Chambersburg PA
CBHW052120110526
44592CB00013B/1682